W9-CEQ-331

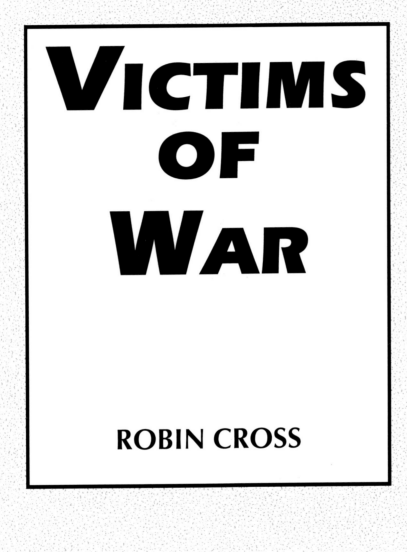

VICTIMS OF WAR

ROBIN CROSS

Thomson Learning

New York

VICTIMS OF WAR

Titles in this series

Propaganda
Victims of War
Women and War
World Leaders

Cover illustration: "The fiend sees your light. Black it out!"

First published in the
United States in 1993 by
Thomson Learning
115 Fifth Avenue
New York, NY 10003

First published in 1993 by
Wayland (Publishers) Limited

Library of Congress Cataloging-in-Publication Data
Cross, Robin
  Victims of war / Robin Cross.
         p.   cm.
  Includes bibliographical references and index.
  Summary: Describes some of the devastating results of World War II, including
refugees, battle fatigue, internment, and destruction of cities.
  ISBN 1-56847-081-9 : $14.95
  1. World War, 1939-1945 Juvenile literature. 2. World War, 1939-1945—
Atrocities—Juvenile literature. 3. Suffering—Juvenile literature. [1. World War,
1939-1945.] I. Title. II. Series: World War Two.
D743.7.C76 1993
940.53--dc20   93-2252

Printed in Italy

Picture acknowledgments

All artwork provided by John Yates.

The publishers would like to thank the
following for allowing their photographs to
be reproduced in this book: Archiv fur
Kunst und Geschichte *cover*, 4, 8, 10, 11,
12, 13, 15, 18, 20, 21, 22, 27, 29, 31, 37,
38, 40, 42, 44; Camera Press 7; Imperial
War Museum 26, 36; Popperfoto 24 both,
25, 28, 33, 35; Topham 9, 34, 39, 43.

Contents

The ravages of war

An estimated 50 million people – soldiers and civilians – died as a result of World War II. Millions more were left wounded in body and spirit. The war brought suffering to the victors and the defeated alike. Of the nations involved in the fighting the Soviet Union was hardest hit, with at least 13 million soldiers killed or missing and more than ten million civilians killed. In just one terrible battle, at Stalingrad, more Russian soldiers were killed than the total number of United States servicemen who died in battle throughout the war.

In Europe and the Far East the war caused forced transfers of populations in which millions died. It pushed civilians into the firing line. They became the targets of enemy bombers and the victims of the cruelest racial and religious persecution.

Two images from the summer of 1945 express the suffering that war brings in its wake: the pathetic, skeletal survivors of Adolf Hitler's concentration camps greeting their Allied liberators; and the blackened, irradiated desert that was left of the Japanese city Hiroshima after an atomic bomb had been dropped on it on August 6, 1945. In the middle of terror and destruction the age of the atom bomb had begun.

An old man in the Warsaw Ghetto in 1941, a victim of Nazi hatred of the Jews. He has collapsed from starvation.

Refugees

On May 10, 1940 Adolf Hitler launched his offensive in western Europe. In the north his Army Group B advanced into Holland. To the south Army Group A thrust through the wooded countryside of the Ardennes. Outflanking the Maginot Line, the French fortification system on the French-German border, the armored spearheads of Army Group A crossed the Meuse River on May 13 and then swung north to trap huge numbers of French and British troops in northern France and Belgium.

The German offensive produced a steady stream of refugees from Belgium fleeing to northern France to escape the fighting. Many of them were wealthy people with cars. A British Army nurse, Moyra Charlton, recalled the arrival of the refugees in Dieppe:

> *Today the town is crowded with refugees from Belgium – cars loaded with the family and luggage, with bicycles strapped on in front and mattresses on the roof for protection against machine gun fire. One had a Belgian flag flying bravely on its bonnet [hood].*[1]

A couple make their way through northern France, fleeing from the fighting.

The speed of the German advance and the scale of the French collapse quickly turned the stream of refugees into a flood. As the Germans closed on Paris millions of people took to the roads, heading south and west of the French capital. By the beginning of June the roads of France were clogged with refugees, the numbers always growing as they moved west. As many as ten million people were on the move.

The Germans did not leave the refugees unscathed. As Moyra Charlton noted, they were in constant fear of German air attack. By harassing the refugees at some points and ignoring them at others, the Germans channeled them onto the roads where they would be most likely to block French troop movements. So the columns of refugees were strafed and bombed and some of the bridges in their path attacked.

After the French surrender on June 22, 1940, the refugees returned to their homes to begin life under the German occupation. In the Far East in May 1942 the Japanese offensive that drove the British army out of Burma produced another tide of refugees. As the British fell back toward India, they were accompanied by hundreds of thousands of Indian, Burmese, and some

Children among a group of Displaced Persons (DPs) at the end of the war, in Meissen in the Soviet-occupied zone of Germany. They had been expelled from their homes in East Prussia.

British civilians. The heavy monsoon rains began long before they reached safety. Major-General H. L. Davies told *Army Quarterly* in 1956: *They died as they walked . . . They died of smallpox, of cholera, of weakness and starvation, or simply of old age – and where they died they lay. No one buried them, they were just pushed off the road and into the verges* [edges] *of the . . . forest, or down the steep banks of the lush ravines below.*[3]

The Japanese did not care about the fate of refugees. After their capture of Hong Kong on December 25, 1941, they drove a million Chinese out of the city so they wouldn't have to feed them. Thousands of the refugees died of starvation. In the last months of the war the Japanese faced their own refugee problem when more than nine million city dwellers – one-seventh of the entire population – fled into the Japanese countryside to escape American bombing. At the end of the war 60 percent of the populations of Japan's six largest cities had fled. This mass migration put a great strain on Japanese society, in which people didn't usually move around the country.

Led by Lieutenant-General Takashu Sakai, troops of the Japanese Twenty-Third Army enter Hong Kong on December 25, 1941. They celebrated their victory by raping and killing thousands of civilians.

At the end of the war there were at least one million refugees in the British-occupied zone of Germany alone. In the summer of 1945 the UNRRA – an agency set up to help refugees – had its work cut out. Every fifth person in the western zones of occupation in Germany was a DP. Many of the UNRRA camps were dangerous places, used as bases by bands of former German prisoners of war (POWs) who roamed the countryside looting and killing. A typical report from the British zone read: 'It is unsafe to work in the fields within eight miles of Adelhaide DP camp owing to the shooting in this area. A total of 1,300 cattle have been looted and slaughtered by the DPs and POWs, quite apart from the atrocious crimes committed by the camp's inhabitants.'

As the war drew to an end in Europe, yet another refugee crisis arose. From 1943 until the war's end waves of refugees washed across Germany, at first fleeing east away from the Allied bombing, and then west away from the advancing Russians. Those fleeing the Russians feared terrible revenge from the Red Army for the cruelty the Germans had inflicted on the Russian people. Some preferred to commit suicide with cyanide pills rather than fall into Russian hands as the Red Army neared Berlin.

By 1948 the number of refugees in Europe had fallen to 550,000, most of them housed in camps in Germany that were run by a new United Nations agency, the International Refugee Organization (IRO).

Many of the Jews who had survived the Nazi Holocaust managed to find a new home in Palestine, which was governed by the British under a United Nations mandate. The British attempted to restrict Jewish immigration to Palestine, and many ships packed with Jews were turned back. In November 1947 the United Nations voted to partition Palestine and form separate Arab and Jewish states. The British left Palestine in May 1948 and Israel, the Jewish state, emerged from the bloodshed of the first Arab-Israeli war.

A column of German refugees trudges through Berlin as the war draws to a close. Millions of refugees were on the move in the summer of 1945.

Battle fatigue and breakdown

In August 1943 the hard-driving U.S. General George S. Patton, commander of the Seventh Army, was touring a tented field hospital in Sicily. He encountered a soldier, fully clothed and slumped on a bed, who had broken down under artillery fire. He told Patton, "It's my nerves. I can hear the shells come over but I can't hear them burst." Patton, an officer who prized physical courage above all else, exploded with rage, calling the man a "coward." Brandishing one of his pearl-handled Colt revolvers, Patton threatened to take the man out and shoot him on the spot. The wretched soldier began to weep. Patton then struck him in the face so violently that the man's helmet liner was knocked off his head and rolled outside the tent. At this point an army medical officer moved in and persuaded Patton to leave. Later, Patton was severely reprimanded by his commander, General Dwight D. Eisenhower, and forced to make a public apology. The soldier he had struck had been suffering from what had previously been called shell shock. In World War II shell shock was named battle fatigue – mental breakdown caused by front-line fighting.

The flamboyant Patton, whose intolerance of battle fatigue nearly destroyed his military career.

German infantry rest on the eastern front in the summer of 1942. With its vast distances and extremes of climate, the U.S.S.R. was an exhausting environment in which to campaign.

In warfare mental wounds are as inevitable as those suffered from bullets and shrapnel. In World War II 10 to 15 percent of British and U.S. battle casualties were cases of mental breakdown. For every five soldiers wounded another was killed and another became a psychiatric casualty. Conditions varied from front to front and from unit to unit. Cases of battle fatigue were sometimes as high as 30 percent and sometimes as low as three percent. Throughout the war it was a serious problem and great efforts were made to find a solution. In 1939 in the Middle East, the British Army had no beds for psychiatric casualties. By March 1943 there were more than 2,000 beds available in the same area, approximately two hospital beds for every 1,000 men.

Battle fatigue is suffered by all combat soldiers, not only those who end up in the hospital. The start of battle fatigue is not sudden, like a bullet wound. It is a final surrender to the terrible strains imposed by fighting, often in extremely harsh physical conditions. Once they are committed to battle, all soldiers set foot on the path to a breakdown. Horror at killing, at seeing their comrades blown apart in front of them, hunger, cold, sleeplessness, and mental exhaustion all take their toll. American soldiers had a name for the empty expression seen on the drawn faces of men exposed to continuous combat, the "2,000-year stare." The writer James Jones, who fought in the Pacific, noted "the staring eyes, slack lips, the sleepwalker's stance" of these men. These were soldiers whose mental and physical resources had been exhausted, to be replaced

A propaganda picture supporting the U.S. daylight bombing offensive against Germany. In reality, by the autumn of 1943 the heavy losses suffered by the American air force led to a slump in morale. German fighter aircraft were shooting down U.S. bombers and their crews faster than they could be replaced. The crisis passed with the arrival of the Mustang long-range escort fighter, capable of accompanying the bombers to and from their targets in the heart of Germany.

by a feeling of "absolute hopelessness." Only the constant flow of replacements and the fact that, at any given time, most men had not yet reached a crisis point kept whole units from being overwhelmed by battle fatigue.

Equally serious was the problem of breakdown among aircrews, particularly those flying bomber aircraft. In the squadrons of Royal Air Force (RAF) Bomber Command an airman's first tour of duty consisted of 30 bombing flights. The first six were considered the most dangerous. After this the crews felt they had some chance of surviving to the end of the tour, although the statistics were not encouraging. It has been calculated that in 1943, when Bomber Command's average monthly loss was running at about four aircraft out of 100, 33 percent of the bomber crews

A U.S. Army survey estimated that almost any soldier, should he survive, would break down after 200 to 250 combat days. The British allowed for 400 days, mainly because their soldiers normally spent shorter periods of time on the front line. As one U.S. soldier confessed: We all get the jitters, especially if it [the fighting] lasts long enough. You get jumpy and want to dive into a hole every time you stop running or walking. You get to think that there might be some pleasure in getting hurt – it would keep you from going nuts.

would survive their first tour. Those who went on a second tour of 25 raids had only a 16 percent chance of completing both tours. Some crews who had been badly shaken up in their first few operations never recovered and fell victim to a failure of nerve known in the RAF as LMF, or "lacking moral fiber." These men were grounded, posted away from the squadron, and sometimes punished by court-martial, lest morale in other crews was undermined. One bomber station commander recalled, "LMF could go through a squadron like wildfire if unchecked."

Few of the airmen who suffered from LMF were cowards. Courage is not an unlimited human quality but something people possess in varying degrees. As Lieutenant Patrick Davies, a British officer who fought in the Far East, recalled: *I do not believe that one man enjoys war after the initial exposure, should that exposure continue for several weeks. The glamour disperses as the tensions prolong, and it is then that ordinary men come close to the heroic. Anyone can be brave once.*

Exhaustion and despair line the face of a German taken prisoner in the winter of 1944.

12

Victims of internment

INTERNMENT IN THE UNITED STATES

At 7:50 a.m. on December 7, 1941, Japanese dive-bombers and torpedo-bombers launched a devastating surprise attack on the great U.S. naval base at Pearl Harbor on the Hawaiian island of Oahu. The next day the U.S. declared war on Japan.

After Pearl Harbor the West Coast was swept by fear of a Japanese invasion. In this climate of shock and anger one group was particularly vulnerable: the 110,000 West Coast residents who were of Japanese origin. Of these about 75,000 were Japanese Americans known as Nisei, or born in the United States.

There was a lull before the storm. Newspapers like the *Los Angeles Times* urged that no vengeful attacks should be made on the Nisei. There should be "no riots, no mob fear." However, the Japanese in western states quickly became the target of public anger. Many people believed that within the Japanese-American community there were numerous spies and saboteurs whose loyalty lay with Japan rather than the U.S. "Once a Jap, always a Jap," they said. The *Los Angeles Times* echoed this mood by changing its earlier moderate tone and saying that the war demanded both the detention of the Japanese and their immediate removal from the West Coast.

The Japanese American Michida family, photographed on their way to an internment camp in the spring of 1942. The children are labeled as if they are just luggage.

The U.S. military was in the forefront of those urging the roundup of the Nisei. Among the public there was a long-held prejudice against Asians, particularly the Japanese. California businessmen eyed the many successful Japanese enterprises they might be able to buy cheaply if their owners were interned by the government and forced to sell. The public mood was turning ugly.

At first the U.S. government considered moving the West Coast Japanese east and dispersing them in the United States interior. On February 19, 1942, 74 days after Pearl Harbor, President Franklin D. Roosevelt signed Executive Order 9066. This gave Secretary of War Henry L. Stimson the authority to designate zones "from which any or all persons may be excluded."

The Japanese were therefore excluded from the West Coast zones. But no one else wanted the Japanese living nearby, so there was nowhere for them to go. Exclusion of the Japanese from the West Coast zones quickly turned into detention. By the end of 1942 all but a handful of Japanese Americans had been confined in ten relocation centers scattered across the U.S. west from the California desert to the swamps of Arkansas. They went peacefully and without protest, taking only what they could carry.

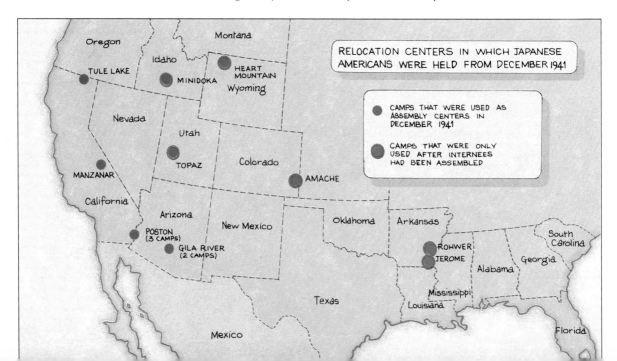

RELOCATION CENTERS IN WHICH JAPANESE AMERICANS WERE HELD FROM DECEMBER 1941

● CAMPS THAT WERE USED AS ASSEMBLY CENTERS IN DECEMBER 1941

● CAMPS THAT WERE ONLY USED AFTER INTERNEES HAD BEEN ASSEMBLED

Oregon
Montana
Idaho
TULE LAKE
HEART MOUNTAIN
MINIDOKA
Wyoming
Nevada
Utah
TOPAZ
Colorado
MANZANAR
AMACHE
California
Arizona
New Mexico
Oklahoma
Arkansas
South Carolina
POSTON (3 CAMPS)
GILA RIVER (2 CAMPS)
ROHWER
JEROME
Georgia
Alabama
Texas
Mississippi
Louisiana
Florida
Mexico

A sandstorm whips through the bleak compound of an internment camp for Japanese Americans at Manzanar in California. At first conditions were very harsh for the internees.

A small number of individuals made legal challenges to the U.S. government's internment program, but these were not upheld by the Supreme Court. As a result, 75,000 American citizens spent the greater part of the war deprived of their civil rights and suffering severe economic hardship.

There had been no compelling military need to herd Japanese Americans into camps. The talk about spy rings and saboteur networks by the U.S. Army after Pearl Harbor proved to be imaginary. By the end of the war nearly 18,000 Japanese Americans had demonstrated their loyalty by serving with the U.S. Army in Europe. The politicians and the legal system had bowed to the pressure of racism and war hysteria. In 1945 Eugene Rostow, a law professor at Yale University, described the internment of the Japanese Americans as the United States' "worst wartime mistake."

By the end of 1944 the West Coast was no longer a war zone. The Japanese Americans were free to go home. Most of them returned to California. In some small towns they were greeted by signs that read "No Japs Allowed." It took many years for them to feel welcome in America once more.

John J. McCloy, a U.S. government official, described the relocation centers as "very good, very pleasant places." This was far from the truth. Consisting of bleak lines of tar-paper huts located in remote, windblown areas, the centers were prisons in all but name, surrounded by barbed wire and armed guards in watch towers. They were built with no thought for the privacy or family lives of their inmates. Life was particularly hard for the young internees, who had seen their parents rounded up by soldiers. One student wrote in an essay: *Since I have been in the camp, I no longer feel I am part of the world. I feel I am a dangerous enemy spy and am being held in prison.*

INTERNMENT IN BRITAIN

In the late 1930s some 70,000 refugees, many of them Jews, had come to Britain from Germany and Austria to escape Nazi persecution. With a German invasion expected daily, these "enemy aliens" were considered a danger to security. The government decided to intern them. When Italy declared war on France on June 10, 1940, Italian citizens living in Britain were also interned.

The government planned to move the internees to the Isle of Man before deporting them to Canada, South Africa, and Australia. In the meantime they were housed in makeshift camps, often in grim conditions. Families were split up without knowing where elderly and sick relations had been sent. For some who had already suffered at the hands of the Nazis, the experience of being rounded up by troops and held behind barbed wire was too much: there were a number of suicides. At the beginning of July a passenger ship, the *Arandora Star*, bound for Canada with 1,500 German and Italian internees, was sunk off the Irish coast by a German submarine. Many of the internees were drowned, among them some who had been well-known opponents of Hitler.

Decency finally won the day. In August 1940 the government's treatment of the internees was heavily attacked in the press and the House of Commons. Release of the internees began almost immediately and soon thousands of them were helping the British war effort, some doing scientific work of the greatest importance.

May 29, 1940: women the British government considers enemy aliens on their way to an internment camp in the Isle of Man.

INTERNMENT IN SOUTHEAST ASIA

In Southeast Asia, the Japanese victories between December 1941 and April 1942 captured thousands of European civilians. Men, women, and children were housed in prisons and camps where life was often brutal and sometimes deadly.

Many civilians had fled from Singapore just before it surrendered to the Japanese Twenty-Fifth Army on February 15, 1942. They had been crammed like cattle into a collection of merchant ships, many of which were sunk by Japanese aircraft and warships in the Bangka Straits. The survivors were washed up on the beaches of Bangka Island. Captured by the Japanese, their next stop was the camp at Muntok on the Sumatran mainland, a place that was to become particularly dreaded and has been described as a "gateway to hell."

The Japanese had nothing but contempt for the defeated colonialists and inflicted endless humiliations on them. The prisoners were compelled constantly to bow to their Japanese captors out of fear of punishment, usually an instant beating. As the end of the war drew near the internees were subjected to near-starvation and the fear that they might all be killed.

This photograph, taken at the end of the war, shows a group of children and a woman in Kampong Makassar, a Japanese internment camp. Many European civilians were imprisoned by the Japanese forces during the war.

Occupation and repression

A Belgian volunteer leaves Antwerp to work in Germany in August 1940.

THE OCCUPATION OF EUROPE

Hitler's empire existed solely to serve Germany's economic interests. In western and central Europe the occupied countries even had to pay the cost of their own occupation. In these countries Hitler created by force a crude forerunner of today's European Community, but one in which the market was fixed entirely in Germany's favor. The occupied countries' food, raw materials, factories, machines, and labor were vital to Germany's war effort. Important industrial concerns were allowed to stay in business under local management, but only if most of their products went to Germany at artificially low prices set by the Germans. This was one-way traffic: Hungarian grain; Danish dairy products; Norwegian timber and bauxite; and the products of French colonies and factories all flowed into Germany. Nothing flowed back. The Germans snatched everything they could and gave back nothing.

In eastern Europe the Germans simply seized what they needed, often leaving nothing behind. In the Soviet Union the industries that had not been sabotaged by the retreating Red Army were taken over by the German Army. The local populations were expected to live at subsistence level. Heinrich Himmler,

AXIS AND AXIS CONTROLLED TERRITORY

AXIS ALLIES

VICHY GOVERNMENT CONTROLLED TERRITORY

GREAT BRITAIN AND POSSESSIONS

NEUTRAL COUNTRIES

GERMAN AND FINNISH ADVANCES INTO SOVIET UNION

chief of the SS (*Schutzstaffel*, or protection squads), the main instrument of Nazi terror, declared: *It is a matter of total indifference to me how the Russians fare . . . Whether the other peoples live in plenty or whether they croak from hunger interests me only to the extent that we need them as slaves for our culture.*

In eastern Europe millions did go hungry. When the Germans were driven out of western Russia in the summer of 1944, they left behind a wasteland. In the countryside and in the ruins of great cities like Minsk, Kiev, and Kharkov, millions lived in pits dug in the ground and roofed over with fir branches. They wore rags, as no new civilian clothes had been available in the Soviet Union since the German invasion in 1941. There was very little food: crops were unsown and huge numbers of cattle had either been slaughtered and eaten by the Germans or driven west ahead of the retreating armies.

In the occupied countries of western Europe daily life was hard. It was almost impossible for civilians to obtain gas or coal, and clothing was severely rationed. In France there was no leather for shoes, so people adopted footwear with wooden soles. The clattering they made on the cobblestones was one of the clearly remembered sounds of the occupation.

At its height in World War II, the German empire stretched from the North Cape of Norway to the Greek island of Crete, and from the Pyrenees on the border between France and Spain to the Caucasus Mountains in the Soviet Union.

People froze in the winter and went hungry all year. Soap shortages led to a fall in hygiene standards and an increase in children suffering from skin diseases like scabies and impetigo. Malnutrition reduced people's resistance to disease, and there were widespread epidemics of tuberculosis, diphtheria, and polio. Restrictions on movement, curfews at night, and the thick wad of identity documents everyone had to carry added to the strain of everyday life.

The greatest European resource plundered by the Germans was a human one – its workers. As the war continued and more Germans went into the armed forces, the need for factory and farm labor increased. Eventually one in every three German men was in the armed forces. At first the Germans attempted to bridge the labor gap with French prisoners of war, of whom there were about one million in Germany. When this failed they tried to recruit workers from occupied countries in the west with offers of good pay and conditions. The pay turned out to be low, the work hard, and the conditions miserable. The Germans then resorted to forced recruitment, and by 1943 there were 12 million foreign workers in Germany. Without them the German war effort would have collapsed. The

A work detail for political prisoners at the German concentration camp at Dachau, near Munich, in 1938. The brutal methods used at Dachau foreshadowed the inhuman treatment of slave labor by the Germans during the war.

Victims of the Lidice massacre, shot by German troops on June 10, 1942 as part of a reprisal for the assassination of Reinhard Heydrich, the Nazi governor of Czechoslovakia.

majority of foreign workers were not volunteers but forced laborers from the East: five million Russian prisoners of war and three million civilians from the Ukraine in western Russia. They were treated like slaves and worked to death, often in factories associated with the concentration and extermination camps. Rudolf Hoess, the commandant of the camp at Auschwitz, estimated of the forced laborers, "In severe working conditions, for instance in mines, every month one-fifth died or were, because of their inability to work, sent back to the camps to be exterminated."

Terror was the Nazis' method of controlling their conquests. Under Hitler's *Nacht und Nebel* (Night and Fog) decree of December 1941, inhabitants of the occupied territories guilty of "endangering German security" were not to be executed immediately but would vanish into the "night and fog" of the unknown. In the hands of the German security services they would be interrogated and tortured by the cruelest methods. In the dungeons of the prison at Breendonk, in Belgium, the SS let starving dogs attack prisoners before they were executed. No information about the prisoners' fate was to be given to their families. Many of these atrocities were carried out by local collaborators recruited by the Germans to persecute their own people. In France a Nazi sympathizer called Joseph Darnand headed a 50,000-strong private army, the *Milice* (Militia), which was as vicious to those who fell into its clutches as the SS.

Under German occupation, which lasted from 1939 to 1944, Poland endured a long nightmare. The Nazis classed Poles as "protected persons" and Polish Jews and gypsies as "reserved persons." But the Poles had no protection. They could not own property. They were forbidden to educate their children beyond primary level. They were barred from their own libraries, theaters, and museums. Movement was so restricted that permission was required to own a bicycle.

The Jews and gypsies were indeed "reserved," but only for the concentration and extermination camps. The German aim was to reduce the entire Polish population to slavery. As the war continued, the Germans systematically got rid of Poland's leading business people, lawyers, church leaders, and educators.

The Germans also retaliated viciously against resistance attacks. In Holland the assassination of a German officer resulted in the deportation of 700 people to concentration camps. On June 4, 1942, SS General Reinhard Heydrich, Himmler's deputy and the Nazi governor of Czechoslovakia, was shot and killed by members of the Czech resistance. In retaliation the villages of Lidice and Lezahy were surrounded by SS soldiers, who shot all the male inhabitants over the age of 16 – 172 men and boys. The women and children were transported to concentration camps. Few survived the war.

THE OCCUPATION OF THE FAR EAST

In Europe the German occupation was based on force and fear; in the Far East the Japanese attempted to put a different face on their empire. In six months of fighting Japanese forces had conquered lands stretching from the Bay of Bengal to the Solomon Sea and containing 150 million people. These people were to become members of what the Japanese called the Greater East Asia Coprosperity Sphere.

Japanese troops round up Chinese prisoners in October 1938. Japan invaded China in July 1937 and systematically exploited the territories over which its armies gained control.

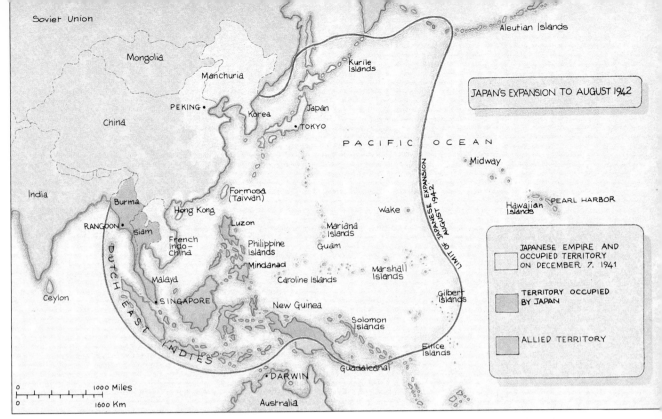

On the map:

Soviet Union
Mongolia
Manchuria
PEKING
China
Korea
Japan
TOKYO
Kurile Islands
Aleutian Islands

JAPAN'S EXPANSION TO AUGUST 1942

PACIFIC OCEAN
Midway
India
Burma
RANGOON
Siam
Hong Kong
Formosa (Taiwan)
Luzon
French Indo-China
Philippine Islands
Mindanao
Wake
Mariana Islands
Guam
Marshall Islands
Caroline Islands
Hawaiian Islands
PEARL HARBOR

LIMIT OF JAPANESE EXPANSION 30 AUGUST 1942

Ceylon
Malaya
SINGAPORE
DUTCH EAST INDIES
New Guinea
Solomon Islands
Gilbert Islands
Ellice Islands
Guadalcanal
DARWIN
Australia

0   1000 Miles
0   1600 Km

JAPANESE EMPIRE AND OCCUPIED TERRITORY ON DECEMBER 7, 1941

TERRITORY OCCUPIED BY JAPAN

ALLIED TERRITORY

At first many of their new subjects welcomed the Japanese, who had driven out the European colonial rulers and had promised "Asia for the Asians." In 1943 Japan declared Burma and the Philippines independent, but it quickly became clear that European imperialism had been replaced by Japanese imperialism. "Coprosperity" actually meant prosperity for Japan alone. Japan's currency, language, and customs were to be forced on the region. Its rich natural resources were taken over by Japanese big business and commandeered for the Japanese war effort. Any resistance was dealt with ruthlessly by the dreaded Japanese military police, the *Kempeitai*.

Massive quantities of food were requisitioned by the Japanese. The price of staple foods like rice skyrocketed. Then supplies dwindled to nothing as American submarines and aircraft sank most of the Japanese merchant shipping fleet, and famine followed. In northern Indochina (now northern Vietnam), a French colony occupied by the Japanese but administered by Vichy, France, more than one million people died of hunger.

The map shows the extent of Japan's expansion into the Pacific up to August 1942.

⟨23⟩

Holocaust

On January 20, 1942, Adolf Hitler made a speech at the Berlin Sports Palace. He told a huge crowd, "The result of the war will be the complete annihilation of the Jews." Anti-Semitism – hatred of the Jews – was a

Right The faces of fear – Polish Jews in the Warsaw ghetto.

Left Smashed Jewish shops in Berlin after an anti-Semitic rampage on the night of November 9, 1938 (known as Kristallnacht), in which 200 synagogues were also burned.

central part of Adolf Hitler's beliefs and of the political philosophy of the Nazi Party he had created in 1920. In his book *Mein Kampf*, published in 1925, Hitler had blamed Jewish Communists for Germany's defeat in World War I.

Before 1939 the Nazis had been content to rob, beat, and drive out the Jews. But the rapid eastward expansion of Hitler's empire, first into Poland in September 1939 and then into the Soviet Union in June 1941, delivered one-third of Europe's Jews into Nazi hands. In Poland about half a million Jews were physically sealed inside the ghetto in Warsaw, the Polish capital. Smaller cities had their own ghettos. No contact was permitted with the outside world, and only the most meager amounts of food were allowed in. Inside the ghettos men, women, and children died on the streets. In 1941 at least 40,000 Jews died of starvation in the Warsaw ghetto.

The scene was set for the mass murder of Jews as an act of deliberate policy. In the summer of 1941, as the German Army drove into the Soviet Union, it was followed by SS *Einsatzgruppen* (Task Groups), whose only job was to kill Jews. Some victims of the *Einsatzgruppen* were rounded up and then shot in trenches that they had been forced to dig; some were gassed in sealed vans filled with carbon monoxide pumped from the van's engine. Between June and November 1941 the four *Einsatzgruppen* operating in western Russia killed nearly a million Jews.

The man who oversaw the Holocaust, Heinrich Himmler, decided that these methods were not efficient enough. A system of camps was devised to speed up the killing. Concentration camps had been a feature of Nazi Germany from the moment Hitler came to power. One of the first, opened in 1933, was at Dachau near Munich. In these detention and forced labor camps the Nazis imprisoned those they considered enemies of the state: Communists, trade union leaders, Catholic priests who had protested against the brutalities of Nazism, Jehovah's Witnesses, homosexuals, and Jews. In the

In 1944 Berlin was declared Judenrein (free of Jews). In fact about 4,000 Jews remained in the city, leading a submerged life that earned them the nickname "U-Boats" (submarines).

Some Jews passed as non-Jews, among them Hans Rosenthal, who became a grave digger. When he dug a grave for two SS officers he told himself that he was "probably the only Jew in Germany who was burying Nazis."

A Polish Jew is executed by a German soldier. The pit below already contains many bodies.

ons antwoord:
Het geweer
ter hand!

Grijpland
Nijpland
Engeland

Vlamingen
alle in de SS Langemarck!

camps these groups were identified by triangles of different colors sewn on their prison wear. Jews wore a yellow triangle, which was later changed to a yellow Star of David.

After 1941, a new type of camp was to implement the Holocaust: the death camp, whose inmates were not expected to live more than 24 hours after their arrival. The first four death camps were built in Poland at Chelmno, Treblinka, Sobibor, and Belzec. They were surrounded by local populations who were as hostile to the Jews as the Nazis. In the ghettos of Poland and across Nazi-occupied Europe the Jews were rounded up, loaded aboard trains, often in cattle trucks, and taken on their one-way journey to the camps. At first they were unaware of the fate that awaited them. They were told that they were to be "resettled" and put to work. Instead they were marched straight off the train and into gas chambers, where they were killed with a cyanide compound, *Zyklon-B*, introduced through vents in the walls.

Opposite page A German anti-Semitic propaganda poster invites Flemish Belgians to join the Langemarck SS Division. The horribly caricatured Jew represents Britain.

Allied liberation by British troops in April 1945 came too late for these inmates of the Belsen concentration camp near Hanover.

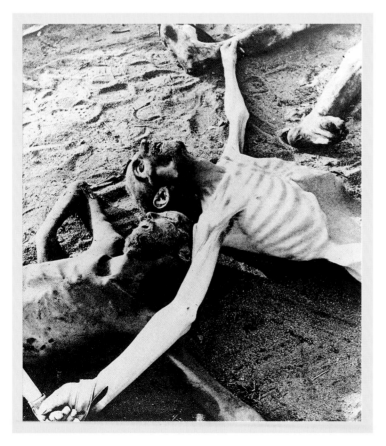

The deception was maintained until the moment of execution. After stripping naked, many of the victims entered the gas chamber believing that they were to be given a shower. At Auschwitz, a camp in southern Poland, the lines outside the gas chambers were made less suspicious by a Jewish band forced to play light classical music.

A small percentage of the able-bodied people who arrived at the camps were not gassed but sentenced to a slower death as slave laborers. In the area around Auschwitz alone, more than 30 factories used slave laborers. When they became too weak to work, they were sent to the gas chambers.

Death itself had become an industry. The commandant of Auschwitz, Rudolf Hoess, took pride in the efficiency with which he ran the camp, where up to 12,000 victims a day were sorted, gassed, and then cremated. Nothing was wasted. The victims' clothes were sold by the SS. The hair clipped from the women's heads by other inmates was used to fill mattresses and make slippers for submarine crews. Gold fillings were removed from the teeth of corpses before they were cremated. At Auschwitz there were also "scientific" experiments of unspeakable cruelty conducted by the camp's senior doctor, Josef Mengele. How long could a man stay in freezing cold water before it killed him? What were the effects of operating without anesthetics? Mengele's smile and soft but deadly touch earned him the nickname "The Angel of Death."

There were those who escaped the Holocaust. The Danes managed to save most of their small Jewish population of 7,000, all but 800 of whom were smuggled into neutral Sweden. The Danish king, Christian X, attended a service in a synagogue to demonstrate his sympathy with the Jews. In the Polish city of Kraków a German Catholic, Oskar Schindler, employed 1,200 Jews from the nearby Plaszow labor camp in his kitchen utensil factory. Under his protection they survived the war, along with 300 women and children Schindler rescued from Auschwitz and another 100 he found on a sealed train.

A most unlikely saint. Oskar Schindler photographed in Israel in 1962 with some of the Jews he saved (see box).

By the end of 1944 about 40 percent of the world's Jewish population, nearly six million men, women, and children, had been put to death. Of the last large European Jewish community, the 800,000 Jews of Hungary, half were handed over to the SS between March and June 1944 and gassed at Auschwitz, the graveyard of at least two million Jews.

By January 1945, four months before the end of the war in Europe, the head of the SS economic branch reported to Himmler that the population of the camps was 714,211, of whom about 202,674 were women. Few of them were Jews, as the Holocaust was almost complete. Before the war there were four million Jews in Poland. When it ended, there were less than 5,000. Those who filled the camps in January 1945 were the other victims of Nazism: Russian prisoners of war, gypsies, political prisoners, and the mentally ill. Indeed, it is likely that the Jews never formed a majority of the population in the camps because many of them were killed as soon as they arrived. Non-Jewish slave laborers, who were kept alive as long as they worked, may have outnumbered them.

The deportation of the Jews was a fact known to almost every adult inhabitant of the continent of Europe between 1942 and 1945. For most people, however,

Preparing for a new life in a new land. Jewish refugees in postwar Germany await the ships that will take them to Palestine (which would be renamed Israel in 1948).

once the Jews were out of sight they were out of mind. Those who tried to help or hide the Jews ran the risk of torture and transportation to the camps if they were discovered or betrayed.

From the early summer of 1942 details of the deportations and the death camps began to filter through to the west, but the scale and horror of the Holocaust only became apparent at the end of the war. As the Red Army advanced into eastern Europe, the SS made clumsy attempts to hide evidence of what they had done. They destroyed the gas chambers and in bitter winter weather marched the thin, starving survivors west to the older concentration camps inside Germany. Many died on the march, and thousands more were killed by starvation and disease at their final destinations. The Allied soldiers who liberated the camps found the dead and dying lying everywhere in heaps, testimony to five years of Nazi terror.

Prisoners of war

At the end of the war in Europe, the U.S. Army had one million German POWs on its hands. It was unable to provide them with even basic shelter. Conditions were dismal: (The enclosures for the reception of prisoners consisted) only of areas of ground surrounded by a single barbed wire fence. Most were completely destitute of any shelter except for scraps of canvas, boards or tin . . . The water supply into the enclosures had either not yet been completed or was completely inadequate. An enclosure at Remagen, designed ultimately to contain 100,000 prisoners, had been only half completed and was occupied by double its capacity. Ten thousand prisoners of war were on sick report at this enclosure . . . Food and medical supplies were extremely short or completely absent. The weather was cold and rainy . . . [7]

The basic rights prisoners of war (POWs) had to humane treatment were detailed in the Geneva Convention of 1929. Prisoners were to be provided with adequate clothing, food, and housing as good as that of their guards, facilities for medical treatment and exercise, and the right to receive letters and gifts of food, clothes, and books. The convention, which was administered by the International Red Cross, forbade physical punishment of prisoners and laid down a maximum penalty of 30 days in solitary confinement for recaptured escapees.

The majority of the nations in World War II had signed the convention. There were two important exceptions: the Soviet Union and Japan. Throughout the war the western Allies applied the terms of the convention to Axis prisoners. In general, the Germans and Italians treated their western prisoners according to the convention. Perhaps the most fortunate POWs of the war were the 175,000 Germans and Italians held in comfortable camps in the U.S. Americans scrupulously followed the terms of the convention and the prisoners were housed and fed in the same way as U.S. troops, a great luxury to many of them.

For British and U.S. POWs in camps run by the Germans the biggest enemy was boredom, but some escapees suffered a harsh fate. On March 24, 1944, 79 Allied airmen escaped from the Stalag Luft III camp at Sagan in Silesia. Of the 73 who were recaptured by the Germans, 50 were executed by the SS on the personal orders of Adolf Hitler.

POWS ON THE RUSSIAN FRONT

Soviet troops were not protected by the Geneva Convention, and the German armies on the eastern front ignored it. Nazi propaganda painted the Soviet soldiers as subhuman figures, and they were treated as such.

The German blitzkrieg on the U.S.S.R. in 1941 produced three million prisoners. The German Army could not house or feed such vast numbers, so they adopted a policy of deliberate neglect. As the chief of the Luftwaffe (air force), Hermann Goering, observed, it would be a positive advantage if "many scores of millions" of Soviets died. The Germans had their plans for the survivors. General Nagel declared, "In contrast to the feeding of other captives [such as British and Americans] we are not obliged to feed the Bolshevik [Soviet] prisoners. Their rations must therefore be determined solely on the basis of their labor performance for us."

A German soldier recalled one of the columns of Soviet prisoners: *From it came a subdued hum, like that of a beehive. Prisoners of war, Russians, six deep . . . We made haste out of the way of the foul cloud which surrounded them, then what we saw transfixed us where we stood and we forgot our nausea. Were these really human beings, these grey-brown figures, these shadows lurching towards us, stumbling and staggering, moving shapes at their last gasp . . . All the misery of the world seemed to be concentrated there.* The picture shows a column of Soviet soldiers who have been captured by Germany in the summer of 1942.

Huge columns of Russian prisoners were marched back to Germany to be used as slave labor. Tens of thousands died of hunger and disease on these forced marches. Those who reached Germany were a pitiful sight. To a British POW, Major Pat Reid, they were like "living skeletons . . . These scarecrows were the survivors of a batch ten times their number which had started from the front. They were treated like animals, given no food and put out into the fields to find fodder amidst the grass and roots."

Winter took a terrible toll on Russian troops whose warm overcoats and fur-lined boots had been stolen by freezing German soldiers. Huddled in barbed-wire cages, often without shelter or heat, thousands of Russian POWs froze to death. During the war nearly six million Soviet troops became POWs, of whom as many as 4.7 million died from shooting, hunger, cold, and forced labor.

German troops captured by the Russians could expect equally harsh treatment. Of the 108,000 Germans who were marched into captivity after the battle of Stalingrad in February 1943, fewer than 5,000 survived the war. On the long march to the prison camp, thousands died of dysentery, cholera, typhus, and starvation. When they arrived at their prison camp the prisoners found that it was "packed with the dead bodies of those who had been taken captive in the Stalingrad South pocket and who had died there of disease. The number of dead was thought to be 42,000 . . . "

Soviet resistance fighters captured by the invading German forces. Soldiers were treated badly by the Germans, but not as badly as resistance members, who were often hung when they were captured.

POWS IN THE FAR EAST

The concept of surrender was shameful to the Japanese. A Japanese soldier expected to die for his emperor, preferring suicide to submission. As a result, comparatively few Japanese were taken prisoner, although the numbers rose toward the end of the war. This feeling that being captured was shameful was reflected in the Japanese treatment of POWs, whom they considered unworthy of respect.

On April 9, 1942, 75,000 American and Filipino troops on the Bataan peninsula in the Philippines surrendered to the Japanese. The Japanese had barely enough supplies for their own troops, so they decided to march their captives some 100 miles to a POW camp at a former U.S. Army barracks. Of those who set out on what became known as the Bataan Death March, only about 55,000 reached the prison camp alive. Thousands more died of hunger and disease in the first few weeks of imprisonment.

Surrendering German soldiers on the eastern front in January 1943. Their clothes are hopelessly inadequate for the Russian winter.

American POWs on the Bataan Death March in the Philippines, April 1942. Twenty-one thousand of those who set out on the march died.

The Japanese treated their prisoners with a mixture of brutality and indifference. POWs and Asian forced laborers were worked to death building the notorious Thai-Burma railroad, which for much of its route ran beside the River Kwai. The railroad was completed in October 1943, but large numbers of POWs were needed to maintain it and repair the damage caused by Allied air raids.

Dressed in rags, the POWs toiled from dawn to dusk in sweltering heat or driving monsoon rains. At night they slept on communal bamboo platforms. There was no medicine to treat tropical diseases. Dysentery was rife and maggot-infested tropical ulcers rotted men's legs until the bone was exposed. Up to 16,000 Allied POWs and at least 100,000 Asian laborers died on the Thai-Burma railroad – one man for every four yards of the track.

Under the bombs

In the 1930s the bomber was seen as a very powerful long-range weapon. In April 1937, at the height of the Spanish Civil War, the bombing of the Basque town of Guernica by aircraft of the German Condor Legion had caused an international outcry. Advocates of air power believed that the next war would be decided in a matter of days as huge air fleets flattened cities in a series of knock-out blows. Their civilian populations, defenseless against air attack, would be seized by mass panic.

The knock-out blow finally fell on London in the late afternoon of September 7, 1940, when the first wave of more than 600 German bombers flew up the Thames River to attack the docks. It was the first night of a bombing campaign that became known as the Blitz. To the men and women of London's fire companies fighting the inferno raging in the warehouses along the Thames it seemed as if "the whole world was on fire."

For the next 56 nights London was bombed from dusk to dawn. After a brief respite the attack was then resumed for another 76 nights. As autumn set in, the Luftwaffe also targeted Britain's major industrial cities and ports, including Birmingham, Bristol, Cardiff, Portsmouth, Southampton, Plymouth, and Hull. Unlike London, however, none of these suffered more than five successive nights of bombing.

Hitler had hoped that the eight million Londoners would be driven mad by the nightly pounding. But the worst fears of the 1930s were not realized. At first civilian morale was badly shaken, but it did not crack. To their amazement Londoners discovered

German bomb damage to London seen from St. Paul's Cathedral, which miraculously survived the Blitz virtually unscathed.

35

A victim of a German V-1 flying bomb attack on London on June 17, 1944. The V-1 offensive began on June 13, 1944 and by March 1945 some 5,500 V-1s, each carrying a one-ton warhead, had hit Britain. The V-1 was followed by the V-2 rocket in September 1944. By the end of the war, V-weapons had killed some 9,000 people and injured 24,500.

that, in spite of the bombs, the routines of life continued. On the morning after a raid that began December 29 and left one-third of London's streets impassable, people still picked their way through the smoking rubble to go to work. Casualties were high but were not measured in hundreds of thousands as had been feared.

Britain's war industries had survived the Blitz, and the inhabitants of the cities under fire had proved that they could take it. This might have prompted the Royal Air Force's Bomber Command to reconsider the effectiveness of the bomber. Instead, it decided that the Germans had simply not done enough bombing. Moreover, the bomber was the only weapon that, at this stage of the war, the British could use to hit Germany directly. From the spring of 1942 the Royal Air Force employed its heavy bomber squadrons against Germany's cities in an area bombing campaign. The bombing offensive was not aimed at individual industrial targets but at the cities in which the German war workers lived. By destroying their homes, or "de-housing" them, the RAF hoped to break the spirit of German civilians and, in turn, undermine the enemy's war industries.

The climax of the area bombing campaign was reached at the end of July 1943 when, in Operation

Corpses piled up haphazardly for cremation after the Allied air raids on the city of Dresden between February 13 and 15, 1945. At the time Dresden was full of refugees and was of no military significance.

Gomorrah, Bomber Command launched four heavy attacks on the city of Hamburg. The United States Eighth Air Force also mounted daylight raids on the city. On the night of July 24, 1943, in the first raid, Bomber Command achieved the principal area bombing objective of swamping Hamburg's civil defenses, blocking the streets, and overstretching the firefighting forces. At one point in the western half of the city it was estimated that 54 miles of buildings were ablaze. During the second heavy raid, on the night of July 27, 729 bombers started a firestorm in eastern Hamburg. High-explosive bombs smashed roofs and blew in windows while fire bombs set buildings ablaze. Floors collapsed and huge tongues of flame burst through the roofs. Then the fires came together, heating the air above and setting up a violent updraft that sucked air from all sides into the center of the fire area. The immense suction created hurricane-force winds that spread the fires as fast as anyone could run, and tossed children and elderly people into the flames.

The experience of Karl-Heinz Alfeis, a 14-year-old, on the night of the third raid on Hamburg, July 29, 1943: People sat and stood, very closely together, in the completely dark air raid shelter. The air got more foul as the ventilation only let in the hot air from the fires outside . . . The shelter received three direct hits . . . One corner of the roof was blown off, but there were no casualties. We survived. When the bombing slackened off, the wardens opened the heavy doors – but what a picture was revealed to our eyes. We lads, now knowing the danger, were the first out. There was a sea of flame as far as we could see. Not one house seemed to be spared. A storm of wind howled through the streets. Bicycles, which had been left outside the shelter, looked like crumpled up balls of wool. It was a desperate sight, all this destruction.[8]

The firestorm engulfed an area almost three miles square and reached its height just before dawn. The dead and dying lay stuck where they fell in the melting asphalt of the streets, their clothes burned away and their bodies shriveled by the heat. The corpses of small children lay on the pavement. In some basement shelters all that was left after the raid was a thin layer of gray ash on the floor, the remains of corpses burned to dust.

The bombing had lasted about an hour, the firestorm four hours more. Most of the 40,000 people killed that night died from heat suffocation or carbon monoxide poisoning, the majority of them long after the RAF bombers had turned for home.

The horror of bombing is dramatically conveyed in this German poster warning of the dangers of not observing the blackout at night. The German caption says, "The fiend sees your light. Black it out!"

U.S. B-29 bombers unleash their loads of high-explosive bombs. As the end of the war in the Pacific drew near, the U.S. used firebombs dropped from B-29s to destroy Japan's major cities.

After the fourth and last raid on Hamburg, on the night of August 2, Albert Speer, the German armaments chief, told Hitler that if another six major German cities were to suffer similar treatment, armaments production would completely break down. But British Bomber Command was unable to keep making such giant raids. Meanwhile, Hamburg recovered. Two-thirds of the city's population had been evacuated after the firestorm, but most of them returned. By December 1943 industrial production had climbed back to 80 percent of normal.

When the war in Europe ended, about 600,000 Germans had been killed by Allied bombing.

As the end of the war approached in the Pacific, the U.S. Army Air Force used fire raids to destroy the cities of Japan. The cities' many wooden buildings made them very vulnerable to attack with fire bombs. On the night of March 9, 1945, 279 American bombers flattened the entire center of Tokyo, destroying 15 square miles of buildings and killing 84,000 people – double the number killed in the eight months of the Blitz on Britain in 1940-41. By the end of May 1945 all the major Japanese cities had been turned into blackened wastelands. More than 200,000 people had been killed or injured.

The wasteland to which the Japanese city of Nagasaki was reduced after the U.S. atomic bomb raid on August 9, 1945.

The thousands of homeless who had not fled into the countryside lived in makeshift shelters in a sea of rubble, warding off starvation by eating weeds.

The war in the Pacific was brought to an end by a new type of bomb. On August 6, 1945 the B-29 Superfortress bomber *Enola Gay* dropped the "Little Boy" atomic bomb on the Japanese city of Hiroshima, killing 100,000 people. Three days later another B-29 dropped the "Fat Man" atomic bomb on Nagasaki, where 75,000 died. People standing by concrete walls near the center of the explosions left no trace but their silhouettes scorched into the concrete by the heat blast, which was blocked for an instant by their bodies before they were vaporized.

On August 15, Japan surrendered. By then radiation sickness was setting in among thousands who had survived the atomic explosions. Most were dead within weeks. In the years that followed thousands more died of leukemia and other radiation-linked cancers. It has been estimated that up to 270,000 citizens of Hiroshima were either killed outright on August 6 or died of radiation sickness within the next five years.

A world in ruins

In May 1945 the countries of Europe were on their knees. Cities like Dresden and Warsaw had been burned to the ground. Almost 90 percent of Warsaw's buildings had been destroyed by the retreating Germans and over half of its population of 1.3 million killed – the equivalent of the combined British and U.S. military losses throughout the war. Along with great cities, small communities had been wrecked by aerial bombardment, artillery shelling, or street battles. At the end of the war the Austrian town of Wiener Neustadt was left with only 18 houses standing and its pre-war population of 45,000 reduced to 860.

The threat of famine hung over Europe. Huge tracts of land had been devastated by flooding, heavy fighting, and "scorched earth" tactics. Shortages of labor, farm machinery, chemical fertilizer, seed, and livestock combined with a severe drought to produce a 1945 grain harvest that was almost 50 percent smaller than that of 1939. In Britain bread rationing was introduced only after the war, in July 1946, because of the need to feed people in the British zone of occupied Germany. A journalist visiting Prague, the capital of Czechoslovakia, wrote: "You don't throw apple cores in the wastebasket here. You fling them out of the window – to be eaten."

A sea of rubble was all that remained of a suburb of the German city of Hamburg in 1945.

The destruction left by the tide of war. Bomb damage in the French port of Calais, June 1940.

The economic prospects were daunting. Coal production in Europe had fallen by nearly 60 percent since 1939. Road, rail, and canal networks were shattered. France had lost two-thirds of its railway locomotives. Ports like Calais, Bordeaux, and Dunkirk were clogged with wreckage. Of the 958 major bridges in the British and American zones in Germany, 740 were destroyed or impassable.

The price of victory had been high. By 1941 the cost of financing the war had virtually bankrupted Britain. For the rest of the war the British decline was concealed by the colossal quantities of goods and raw materials shipped across the Atlantic by the United States under the terms of the Lend-Lease Act of 1941. When Lend-Lease ended in 1945, the British government had debts it could not pay. Economic collapse was stopped only by an emergency loan from the United States.

The Soviet Union finished the war as the strongest military power in Europe, but it was a crippled giant. About one-quarter of all property in the Soviet Union had been destroyed during the war, and more than 2,000 towns and 70,000 villages now existed only on maps. Nearly 2.5 million Russian civilians had been killed in the war and 25 million of the population were homeless.

In contrast the U.S., which had been physically untouched by the war, emerged as the economic powerhouse of the West. In 1939 the U.S. was still shrugging off the effects of the Great Depression. Mobilization for war produced an economic surge that released the vast power of American industry. By 1944 it was producing 40 percent of the world's armaments. One Ford plant alone employed 42,000 people. Wages and living standards here rose during the war, bringing a new prosperity to farmers and factory workers alike. Between 1940 and 1945 the farmers' cash income increased by more than four times; the weekly wages of industrial workers rose by 70 percent.

In the occupied countries liberated by the Allies reprisals were taken against those who had collaborated with the Germans. In France the process was known as the "purification." Between September 1944 and December 1949, 170,000 French citizens were brought to trial for collaborating with the enemy. Just over 120,000 received sentences, of which 4,785 were death penalties. In the end there were 2,000 executions. All death sentences on minors and women were reduced to terms of imprisonment by General Charles de Gaulle, who was provisional president of France until January 1946. However, the French Resistance settled many old scores without resorting to the courts, executing as many as 50,000 in the chaotic weeks following the liberation. Women who had slept with Germans were punished by having their heads shaved.

In the middle of Europe lay defeated Germany. Bombing had gouged the heart out of its cities and industries. For every ton of bombs dropped on Britain by the Luftwaffe, 347 tons had been dropped on Germany. One house in every three had been destroyed.

Through the rubble-strewn streets of Berlin shuffled an army of zombies, thousands of German soldiers, their overcoats tied with string and their feet wrapped in sacking. After the German surrender on May 7, 1945, the people of Berlin were struggling to survive on a diet of about 800 calories a day: humans should have about 2,500 calories a day. In March 1946 the ration in the British-occupied sector of Berlin dropped to 400 calories a day, less than that which the Nazis had given the inmates of concentration camps.

There were virtually no medical supplies: in the British sector of Berlin, 43 of the 44 hospitals had

A Frenchwoman at the end of the war, having her head shaved as a punishment for collaboration.

The journalist Tom Pocock toured the Russian sector of Berlin in July 1945. He noted: *here and there, bared steel girders like warped climbing frames in a children's playground . . . Sometimes we passed . . . lines of women carrying buckets, waiting outside the less ruined buildings, where the Allied troops had already been billeted, in the hope of being given a swill of leftovers after the soldiers had eaten.*[10]

been destroyed or badly damaged. Burst water mains and broken sewers spread typhoid and dysentery. In July 1945 six out of every ten babies born in Berlin died of dysentery.

Outside the makeshift medical facilities, the ruins of the city hid an even deadlier danger than disease. Berlin's streets were full of unexploded ammunition – shells, mines, and grenades of which more than 1,500 tons were recovered every day. The rubble with which Berlin was rebuilt was sifted by gangs of women, as most of the men were either dead or prisoners of war.

Adolf Hitler had committed suicide in his Berlin bunker on April 30, 1945. His main legacy was the division of Europe between East and West. Under the Marshall Aid Plan, western Europe slowly recovered from the ravages of war with the help of billions of dollars from the U.S. Central and Eastern Europe fell under a harsh Soviet domination. Poland, for which the French and British had gone to war in September 1939, exchanged Nazi tyranny for Soviet control. Elsewhere in the new Soviet empire Joseph Stalin ensured that the new governments were friendly to the Soviet Union. Only one hole remained in the Iron Curtain that had descended across Europe. In Russian-occupied East Berlin people could buy an underground railway ticket to West Berlin and go from there to West Germany. Berlin became the focus of a struggle for the control of central Europe between the U.S. and the U.S.S.R. that was to last until the fall of the Berlin Wall in 1989 and the collapse of the Soviet Union.

Storm clouds gather over the ruins of the German city of Nuremberg at the end of the war. It had been pounded by Allied heavy bombers.

Glossary

Alien   Someone who is not a legal citizen of the country in which he or she lives.

Axis   The powers allied to Germany during World War II – Italy (until 1943) and Japan.

Blitzkrieg   "Lightning war." A term coined to describe the German tactic of waging war with rapid thrusts by tanks supported by aircraft. Employed for the first time in the invasion of Poland in 1939.

Collaborator   A person who helps an enemy army that has taken over his or her country by force.

Emigration   Leaving one's native land to live in another country.

Gestapo   The Nazi secret police, much feared because of their use of torture.

Ghetto   An isolated or segregated area in a city inhabited by a minority group, usually poor. Originally applied to Jewish areas.

Great Depression   During the early 1930s the U.S. entered a period of high unemployment that left many people homeless and poor. This Great Depression affected the rest of the world, as goods could no longer be sold to the U.S. and loans from U.S. banks had to be repaid.

Gypsy   A person who does not live in a fixed place but travels around with all of his or her possessions. In the past, because they were different from other people and often did not want to mix with them, gypsies were disliked.

Internment   The imprisonment of aliens, prisoners of war, or suspected saboteurs.

Isthmus   A neck of land between two seas.

Lend-Lease   An act passed by the U.S. Congress in March 1941, before the U.S. entered the war, which allowed democratic countries to borrow war supplies from the U.S. in return for services and goods.

Marshall Aid Plan   A huge postwar aid package from the U.S. to Europe. Officially known as the European Recovery Program, it was popularly known as the Marshall Aid Plan after General George C. Marshall, the U.S. Secretary of State whose idea it was.

Puppet leader   A head of government appointed by another country to do as it wants.

Repatriation   The official return of an individual to his or her own country.

Scorched earth   The deliberate burning, destruction, and removal by an army of everything – food, shelter, factories – that could be used by an enemy advancing into the area.

Silesia   Part of Poland around the basin of the Oder River, which was regained from Germany in 1945.

SS   Abbreviation for *Schutzstaffel* (Protection Detachment). Originally Hitler's personal bodyguard, the SS became very powerful. SS men ran the concentration and extermination camps, supervised the mass deportations, and imposed Hitler's will throughout Europe with the greatest brutality. The *Waffen* (Armed) SS provided military units that fought alongside the German Army.

Strafe   To fire upon at close range.

Synagogue   Jewish place of worship.

Books to read

Allen, Peter. *The Origins of World War II.* Witness History. New York: Bookwright Press, 1992.

Frank, Ann. *Ann Frank: The Diary of a Young Girl.* New York: Doubleday, 1967.

Friedman, Ina R. *The Other Victims: First-Person Stories of Non-Jews Persecuted by the Nazis.* Boston: Houghton Mifflin, 1990.

Landau, Elaine. *Nazi War Criminals.* International Affairs. New York: Franklin Watts, 1990.

Rossel, Seymour. *The Holocaust: The Fire that Raged.* Venture Books. New York: Franklin Watts, 1989.

Stein, R. Conrad. *Prisoners of War.* World at War. Chicago: Childrens Press, 1987.

Sources of quotations
1 & 2 *Unsung Heroines,* Vera Lynne with Robin Cross and Jenny de Gex (Sidgwick and Jackson, 1990). **3** Major-General H. L. Davies in *Army Quarterly,* 1956. **4 & 5** *Normandy Revisited,* A. J. Leibling (Victor Gollancz, 1959). **6** Quoted in *Where Did the Forties Go?*, Andrew Davies (Pluto Press, 1984). **7** Quoted in *Prisoner of War,* Major Pat Reid (Grub Street, 1984). **8** *The Battle of Hamburg: The Firestorm Raid,* Martin Middlebrook (Penguin, 1984). **9** *New Yorker Magazine.* **10** *1945: The Dawn Came Up Like Thunder,* Tom Pocock (Collins, 1983). The account on page 9 of Patton's assault on a soldier suffering battle fatigue is quoted in *World War II: The Sharp End,* John Ellis (Windrow and Greene, 1990)